Lerner **SPORTS**

GREATEST OF ALL TIME PLAYERS

G.O.A.T. BASKETBALL
POWER FORWARDS

Alexander Lowe

Lerner Publications ◆ Minneapolis

SPORTS THRILLS
MEET
RESEARCH SKILLS

Lerner SPORTS

Free Database Trial: **lernersports.com**

Lerner Publications Company
An imprint of Lerner Publishing Group, Inc.
241 First Avenue North
Minneapolis, MN 55401 USA

For reading levels and more information, look up this title at www.lernerbooks.com.

Main body text set in Aptifer Sans LT Pro.
Typeface provided by Linotype AG.

Library of Congress Cataloging-in-Publication Data
Names: Lowe, Alexander, author.
Title: G.O.A.T. basketball power forwards / Alexander Lowe.
Other titles: Greatest Of All Time basketball power forwards
Description: Minneapolis, MN : Lerner Publications , [2023] | Series: Greatest Of All Time Players (Lerner Sports) | Includes bibliographical references and index. | Audience: Ages 7–11 years | Audience: Grades 2–3 | Summary: "Basketball's greatest power forwards can score from the three-point line, next to the basket, and everywhere in between. See how the top 10 power forwards in basketball history rank. Then rank them yourself!"— Provided by publisher.
Identifiers: LCCN 2021059798 (print) | LCCN 2021059799 (ebook) | ISBN 9781728458052 (Library Binding) | ISBN 9781728463223 (Paperback) | ISBN 9781728461342 (eBook)
Subjects: LCSH: Forwards (Basketball)—United States—Biography—Juvenile literature. | Basketball players—Rating of—Juvenile literature.
Classification: LCC GV884.A1 L6946 2023 (print) | LCC GV884.A1 (ebook) | DDC 796.323092/2 [B]—dc23/eng/20220201

LC record available at https://lccn.loc.gov/2021059798
LC ebook record available at https://lccn.loc.gov/2021059799

Manufactured in the United States of America
1 – CG – 7/15/22

TABLE OF CONTENTS

FABULOUS FORWARDS

The Milwaukee Bucks were playing the Phoenix Suns in Game 4 of the 2021 National Basketball Association (NBA) Finals. The Bucks had a two-point lead with just over one minute left in the game.

Suns point guard Devin Booker dribbled toward the basket. Bucks power forward Giannis Antetokounmpo ran at him to stop Booker from scoring. Booker threw the ball toward the basket for teammate Deandre Ayton, who jumped for a slam dunk.

FACTS AT A GLANCE

» **CANDACE PARKER** WAS THE FIRST WOMAN TO APPEAR ON THE COVER OF THE *NBA2K* VIDEO GAME.

» **TIM DUNCAN** WON FIVE NBA CHAMPIONSHIPS.

» **PAU GASOL** WON TWO SILVER MEDALS IN THE OLYMPIC GAMES WHILE PLAYING FOR THE SPAIN NATIONAL TEAM.

» **DIRK NOWITZKI** IS RANKED SIXTH IN POINTS SCORED IN NBA HISTORY.

Antetokounmpo reacted to the pass. He quickly switched directions and jumped. His timing was perfect, and he stopped the dunk with a block off the backboard. The Bucks won the game and would go on to win the Finals.

Good power forwards are some of the best players on a basketball team. They must be big enough to guard the basket and grab rebounds. They must also be skilled enough to shoot the ball from outside and dribble the ball up the court.

Candace Parker (*left*) was the first pick of the 2008 Women's National Basketball Association Draft.

Tim Duncan (*left*) won five NBA championships during his playing career.

Power forwards are usually some of the biggest players on the court. They often play near the basket, but they are usually smaller and quicker than centers. Some power forwards are known for their scoring skills. Others are better at playing defense, blocking shots, and grabbing rebounds. The greatest power forwards in NBA history can do it all.

PAU GASOL

Pau Gasol is one of the most skilled power forwards in the history of the NBA. He was an excellent shooter and one of the first big players to have that ability. At 7 feet (2.1 m) tall, it was nearly impossible for defenders to stop Gasol from sinking long-range shots and scoring close to the basket.

Gasol won two straight NBA titles with the Los Angeles Lakers in 2009 and 2010. With teammate Kobe Bryant, the Lakers had the two best superstars in the NBA. Gasol joined the Chicago Bulls after leaving the Lakers and had some of his best defensive years there. In the 2014–2015 season, he averaged a career high of 11.8 rebounds per game.

Gasol had an impact on the game around the world. He won two Olympic silver medals in 2008 and 2012 and a bronze medal in 2016 while playing for Spain's national team.

PAU GASOL STATS

Points Per Game	17
Blocks Per Game	1.6
Rebounds Per Game	9.2
Assists Per Game	3.2

KEVIN MCHALE

Kevin McHale was one of the first players in the NBA to turn scoring in the post into an art. The post is the area near the sides of the basket. McHale used spin moves, quick shots, and strength to score in bunches. His skills helped lead the Boston Celtics to three NBA championships during his career.

McHale's scoring really made him stand apart from other players. His shooting accuracy was incredible for a player of his size. In his career, he made 55 percent of the shots he took.

For most of his career, McHale started games on the bench. He came into games later and still found a way to help his team. He had the ability to guard other power forwards, but he could also match up well against centers and small forwards. He was one of the most skilled players of the 1980s.

KEVIN MCHALE STATS

🏀	Points Per Game	17.9
🏀	Blocks Per Game	1.7
🏀	Rebounds Per Game	7.3
🏀	Assists Per Game	1.7

Lauren Jackson is one of the most complete players in the history of the Women's National Basketball Association (WNBA). She could shoot. She could defend. Most of all, she could block shots. At 6 feet, 6 inches (1.98 m), Jackson was one of the tallest players in the league. She used her height to her advantage and spent six seasons in the top three in the league for blocks.

From 2003 to 2010, Jackson was the best player in the WNBA. She was selected to the All-WNBA team eight times. Jackson won three Most Valuable Player (MVP) awards and a Defensive Player of the Year award. Most importantly, Jackson led her team to two WNBA championships.

When Jackson retired, she was ranked 10th in league history for scoring and fifth in blocks. She was the scoring champion of the league three times. Her skill on offense and defense made her a dominant force in the WNBA.

LAUREN JACKSON STATS

Points Per Game	18.9
Blocks Per Game	1.8
Rebounds Per Game	7.7
Assists Per Game	1.4

Dirk Nowitzki grew up in Germany. He came to the NBA in 1998 to play for the Dallas Mavericks. Nowitzki spent his entire career with the Mavericks. In 21 seasons with the team, he scored 31,560 points. He also made 1,982 three-point shots.

Nowitziki was a great scorer. He could shoot the ball from anywhere on the court. He held the ball high when he took a shot, making him very difficult to defend. He retired from the NBA as the sixth-leading scorer in NBA history.

The highlight of his career was in the 2011 NBA Finals. The Miami Heat were favored to win, thanks to superstars LeBron James and Dwyane Wade. But Nowitzki and the Mavericks beat the Heat on Miami's home court. For his outstanding performance, he won the Finals MVP award.

DIRK NOWITZKI STATS

Points Per Game	20.7
Blocks Per Game	0.8
Rebounds Per Game	7.5
Assists Per Game	2.4

Charles Barkley was best known for his rebounding ability. He was shorter than many other power forwards in the NBA. But Barkley made up for it with skill, strength, and smart play. Barkley is one of the greatest rebounders in NBA history.

Barkley was also skilled at making plays and scoring points. When it came to dribbling, passing, and shooting, few forwards could compete with him. He was the fourth player in NBA history to reach 20,000 points, 10,000 rebounds, and 4,000 assists in his career.

Barkley won a gold medal with Team USA at the 1992 Olympics as part of the Dream Team. The Dream Team was packed with NBA players. Fans consider it one of the greatest sports teams ever. Barkley was the highest-scoring member of the team.

He ended his career as an 11-time All-NBA team player. Barkley was also an NBA All-Star 11 times and won the league MVP award in 1993. Barkley retired after the 1999–2000 season, but he still ranks 20th in league history in rebounds.

CHARLES BARKLEY STATS

Points Per Game	22.1
Blocks Per Game	0.8
Rebounds Per Game	11.7
Assists Per Game	3.9

KARL MALONE

Karl Malone has the second most points of any player in NBA history. He averaged more than 25 points per game for 12 of his first 15 seasons in the league. The only seasons he did not average more than 20 points per game were his first and his last.

Malone and point guard John Stockton helped make the Utah Jazz one of the best teams in the NBA throughout the 1990s. Fans got used to seeing Stockton throw the ball to Malone in the post so Malone could go to work. As a result, the Jazz were always near the top of the league.

NBA fans, reporters, and players voted for Malone to play in 14 All-Star Games. He also won the league MVP award twice. Malone is one of only two players in NBA history to be an All-NBA team player in 11 straight seasons.

KARL MALONE STATS

🏀	Points Per Game	25
🏀	Blocks Per Game	0.8
🏀	Rebounds Per Game	10.1
🏀	Assists Per Game	3.6

Giannis Antetokounmpo is one of the most gifted players in the history of the NBA. He is tall, standing at 6 feet, 11 inches (2.1 m). He is fast, moving from one end of the court to the other much faster than most players his size. His speed and strength make him nearly impossible to stop.

The Milwaukee Bucks chose Antetokounmpo with the 15th overall pick in the 2013 NBA Draft. Since he had grown up in Greece, many US fans had never heard of him. Within a few years, he was one of the best players in the league. In 2019, he won his first of two league MVPs. In 2021, he won the NBA Finals MVP award when he helped the Bucks win the league championship.

Antetokounmpo's stats are already impressive, and his career is just getting started. Some fans think that by the time he retires, he could be the greatest power forward of all time.

GIANNIS ANTETOKOUNMPO STATS

Points Per Game	21
Blocks Per Game	1.3
Rebounds Per Game	9.2
Assists Per Game	4.5

Stats are accurate through December 15, 2021.

Candace Parker was a great player from the minute she stepped onto a WNBA court. In 2008, she became the first player in WNBA history to win both the Rookie of the Year and MVP awards in the same season. She has played at a high level ever since.

Parker's best season came in her third year. She averaged 20.6 points and 10.1 rebounds per game. She did all this while making 50 percent of her shots.

Parker won the league MVP award twice. She also was the WNBA Finals MVP in 2016. As her career went on, she became an even better defender. In 2020, she became the Defensive Player of the Year. After the 2021 season, she was seventh in WNBA history in rebounds and sixth in blocks. Thanks to her strength on the court, in 2021 she became the first woman to appear on the cover of the *NBA2K* video game.

CANDACE PARKER STATS

🏀	Points Per Game	16.6
🏀	Blocks Per Game	1.6
🏀	Rebounds Per Game	8.6
🏀	Assists Per Game	4

Stats are accurate through the 2021 WNBA season.

KEVIN GARNETT

Kevin Garnett is the best defender to ever play the power forward position. He played with an intense style that frustrated other teams for years. He had the strength to leap and block any shot. He also had the speed to run with much smaller players as they tried to drive to the basket.

Garnett was also a very skilled offensive player. He was a great scorer and an expert passer. Garnett helped run his team's offense from the post. Defenders never knew if he was going to drive to the basket for a slam dunk, pull up for a quick shot, or pass the ball to an open teammate.

Garnett won the NBA MVP award for the 2003–2004 season and the Defensive Player of the Year award in 2007–2008. He earned a place on 15 All-Star teams and nine All-NBA teams. Garnett's great play at both ends of the court makes him one of the greatest power forwards of all time.

KEVIN GARNETT STATS

Points Per Game	17.8
Blocks Per Game	1.4
Rebounds Per Game	10
Assists Per Game	3.7

TIM DUNCAN

Tim Duncan was a winner. In 1999, he helped lead the San Antonio Spurs to the NBA title. But he was just getting started. Duncan and the Spurs won championships in 2003, 2005, 2007, and 2014. Few other teams have ever matched their success.

Duncan was not a flashy player. He worked hard, stayed calm on the court, and made smart plays. He was a strong rebounder and a great scorer. When he got the ball in the post, no one could keep him away from the basket.

Duncan played like a superstar for 19 NBA seasons. He was an All-Star 15 times. He also made 15 All-NBA and All-Defensive teams. Duncan won two league MVP awards and three NBA Finals MVPs. Very few players have won that many honors and awards. Duncan's personal and team success make him the greatest power forward of all time.

TIM DUNCAN STATS

Points Per Game	19
Blocks Per Game	2.2
Rebounds Per Game	10.8
Assists Per Game	3

EVEN MORE G.O.A.T.

There have been many other great players who played power forward. Narrowing the list to the 10 greatest of all time is really tough. Here are 10 more players who nearly made the G.O.A.T. list.

....

No. 11   BOB PETTIT

No. 12   YOLANDA GRIFFITH

No. 13   ELVIN HAYES

No. 14   DENNIS RODMAN

No. 15   NNEKA OGWUMIKE

No. 16   REBEKKAH BRUNSON

No. 17   JERRY LUCAS

No. 18   ANTHONY DAVIS

No. 19   CHRIS WEBBER

No. 20   AMAR'E STOUDEMIRE

YOUR G.O.A.T.

It's your turn to make a G.O.A.T. list about power forwards. Start by doing research. Consider the rankings in this book. Then check out the Learn More section on page 31. Explore the books and websites to learn more about basketball players of the past and present.

You can search online for more information about great players too. Check with a librarian, who may have other resources for you. You might even try reaching out to basketball teams or players to see what they think.

Once you're ready, make your list of the greatest players of all time. Then ask people you know to make G.O.A.T. lists and compare them. Do you have players no one else listed? Are you missing anybody your friends think is important? Talk it over and try to convince them that your list is the G.O.A.T.!

GLOSSARY

All-Defensive team: a team made up of the best defenders from each NBA season

All-NBA team: an honor given to the 15 best players from the NBA season

All-WNBA team: an honor given to the 15 best players from the WNBA season

assist: a pass from a teammate that leads directly to a score

blocked shot: when the ball is knocked away by a defender before reaching the basket

center: a player who usually stays close to the basket and the middle of the court

Finals: the NBA's championship series

point guard: the player who leads a basketball team on offense

post: an area on a basketball court that is located just outside the free throw lane near the basket

rebound: grabbing and controlling the ball after a missed shot

slam dunk: a shot in basketball made by jumping high into the air and throwing the ball down through the basket

LEARN MORE

Candace Parker
https://www.sikids.com/tag/candace-parker

Labrecque, Ellen. *All-Time Best WNBA Players*. Mankato, MN: The Child's World, 2020.

Leed, Percy. *Tim Duncan: Power Forward*. Minneapolis: Lerner Publications, 2022.

Power Forward (Basketball) Facts for Kids
https://kids.kiddle.co/Power_forward_(basketball)

Scheff, Matt. *NBA and WNBA Finals: Basketball's Biggest Playoffs*. Minneapolis: Lerner Publications, 2021.

Tim Duncan
https://kids.britannica.com/students/article/Tim-Duncan/311079

INDEX

PHOTO ACKNOWLEDGMENTS

Image credits: Jonathan Daniel/Staff/Getty Images, p.4; Stacy Revere/Staff/Getty Images, p.5; Mike Mattina/Stringer/Getty Images, p.6; Stephen Dunn/Staff/Getty Images, p.7; Stephen Dunn/Staff/Getty Images, p.8; Gregory Shamus/Staff/Getty Images, p.9; SportsChrome/Newscom, p.10; Staff/Getty Images, p.11; Christian Petersen/Staff/Getty Images, p.12; Christian Petersen/Staff/Getty Images, p.13; Ronald Cortes/Stringer/Getty Images, p.14; Ronald Martinez/Staff/Getty Images, p.15; John McDonough/Icon SMI/Newscom, p.16; John W. McDonough/Icon SMI/Newscom, p.17; Jed Jacobsohn/Staff/Getty Images, p.18; Otto Greule Jr/Stringer/Getty Images, p.19; Stacy Revere/Staff/Getty Images, p.20; Stacy Revere/Staff/Getty Images, p.21; Jonathan Daniel/Staff/Getty Images, p.22; Christian Petersen/Staff/Getty Images, 23; Jared Wickerham/Staff/Getty Images, p.24; Image of Sport/Image of Sport Photos/Newscom, p.25; Chris Covatta/Stringer/Getty Images, p.26; Streeter Lecka/Staff/Getty Images, p.27

Cover: Streeter Lecka/Staff/Getty Images; Harry How/Staff/Getty Images; Christian Petersen/Staff/Getty Images